G000163270

THE SECOND WORLD WA
IN PHOTOGRAPHS

1939

L. ARCHARD

AMBERLEY

03447677

Acknowledgements

This book would not have been possible without the kindness of Campbell McCutcheon, who granted permission to use images from his collection. Unless otherwise indicated, images are from the J. & C. McCutcheon Collection. Other images are courtesy of John Christopher (JC), Wikipedia, the Amberley Archive (AA) and the Library of Congress (LoC).

First published 2014

Amberley Publishing
The Hill, Stroud
Gloucestershire, GL5 4EP

www.amberley-books.com

Copyright © L. Archard 2014

The right of L. Archard to be identified as the Author
of this work has been asserted in accordance with the
Copyrights, Designs and Patents Act 1988.

All rights reserved. No part of this book may be reprinted
or reproduced or utilised in any form or by any electronic,
mechanical or other means, now known or hereafter invented,
including photocopying and recording, or in any information
storage or retrieval system, without the permission in writing
from the Publishers.

British Library Cataloguing in Publication Data.
A catalogue record for this book is available from the British Library.

ISBN 978 1 4456 2234 7 (print)
ISBN 978 1 4456 2257 6 (ebook)

Typeset in 10pt on 12pt Sabon.
Typesetting and Origination by Amberley Publishing.
Printed in the UK.

Introduction

On 1 September 1939, German forces crossed the border and invaded Poland. The British and French governments had guaranteed Polish independence on 2 March that year and issued Germany with an ultimatum to withdraw its forces. Historians have argued that Hitler had not wanted a general European conflict in 1939, and that he had assumed that Britain and France would not act to stop him, as they had not when he remilitarised the Rhineland, when the Anschluss with Austria was declared, when the Sudetenland had been annexed and when German forces had invaded the rest of Czechoslovakia. However, Chamberlain had been outraged by the way in which Hitler had broken his word over Czechoslovakia, and had decided, along with the French government, to make a stand over Poland.

The result was that, when the ultimatum expired at 11 a.m. on 3 September, Chamberlain addressed the nation and declared war on Germany. When war had been declared in 1914, there had been a febrile atmosphere, with huge crowds gathering outside Buckingham Palace, but in 1939 the pervading mood was quiet dread. This was partly due to the memory of the First World War, and partly due to a sense that things had moved on dramatically, particularly in terms of war in the air. The 1930s in particular had seen the dominance of the idea that 'the bomber will always get through': massed formations of aircraft carrying both heavy bomb-loads and strong defensive armaments would be able to break through any defences. What the bombers would do when they reached their target could be seen in newspaper reports from Guernica, Shanghai and Chunking, to name three examples. These news reports, along with the words of Bertrand Russell and H. G. Wells among others, had done much to fuel pacifism.

Guernica is one of the most famous examples of the use of air power against a civilian population. The town was of great symbolic importance to the Basques, who were fighting as part of the Republican forces in the Spanish Civil War to gain more independence from Madrid. On 26 April 1937, a market day, aircraft of the Condor Legion (the German forces fighting alongside General Franco's Nationalists) attacked the town in two waves; the first, of eighteen aircraft, attacked from low level; the second wave dropped incendiary bombs from high altitude, setting the whole town alight. The attack on Guernica won great sympathy for the Republicans from around the world; in a report quoted in Len Deighton's *Blood, Tears and Folly*, a German staff officer later noted that the attack had strengthened Basque resistance rather than breaking it and that, unsurprisingly, the Basques were now anti-German.

German involvement in the Spanish Civil War on the side of the Nationalists had begun almost immediately; very soon after the military uprising that began the war, emissaries of General Franco had sought out Hitler at the Wagner Festival in Bayreuth to appeal for German aid. Göring provided twenty Ju-52 transport aircraft to carry soldiers of the Spanish Foreign Legion from Morocco to the Spanish mainland; the Ju-52s transferred some 3,000 soldiers in one day. A few months later, the Germans would also provide fighters, more Junkers 52s adapted as bombers, reconnaissance aircraft, seaplanes and anti-aircraft units, as well as Luftwaffe personnel technically designated civilian volunteers. The Italians also provided aircraft and personnel to help the Nationalists, while the USSR provided similar help for the Republican forces.

The Germans quickly discovered that their Heinkel 51 biplane fighters were inferior to the I-16 monoplane fighters provided by the Russians, and phased them out. Using loose formations of fighters, however, a tactic pioneered by the Germans, proved superior to the Republican tactics. Messerschmitt 109Bs were taken to Spain and when the I-16s proved a match for these too, the lessons learned were incorporated into the design of the 109E, which appeared during the final weeks of the war. Both the German He 111 and the Russian SB-2 had been able to escape from enemy fighters and flak by virtue of sheer speed. Most significantly, strategic bombing was discouraged in Spain as neither side was keen for the towns they fought for to be annihilated. The Condor Legion was forced to do what the Nationalist army wanted and air power was subordinated to army commanders, leading to close cooperation between ground and air forces.

There was an earlier sign of things to come in January 1932, when the Japanese navy attacked Shanghai. Nationalism and militarism had become increasingly important in Japan following the Great Depression, and war had broken out with the invasion of Manchuria (in north-eastern China) in September 1931. The attack on Shanghai was an extension southwards of the war with China. The day after the invasion of the city's Chapei district by Japanese marines, carrier-borne aircraft bombed the area, which was heavily populated by Chinese civilians. This was the first major instance of the bombing of civilians and, like Guernica, happened in full view of the world's press. The Japanese commander, Admiral Shiozawa, resented being described as a 'Babykiller' in the American newspapers, pointing out to a journalist that he should be given credit for only using 30-lb bombs when he might have used 500-lb bombs instead. A treaty was signed and formally there was peace again.

However, on 7 July 1937 war broke out again following an 'incident' at the Marco Polo Bridge just outside Peking. Among many other towns and cities, Shanghai was attacked again from the air before it fell to Japanese forces. Air attacks on Chinese cities were commonplace, but a raid in May 1939 on the city of Chungking, to which the Chinese leader Chiang Kai-shek had moved his capital, provoked particular horror. The city was particularly vulnerable because it stood on the confluence of two rivers, the Yangtze and the Chialing, which made it easy to find from the air. The bombers arrived at dusk on the night of an almost full moon and caused havoc in the city, which was full of refugees; the attack happened when the streets were crowded with people on their way home from work, resulting in 7,000 casualties.

For Britain, then, September 1939 was a month of preparation for the heavy bombing of civilian populations. The first event of the Second World War for many

Londoners came almost immediately after Chamberlain's declaration of war when a French civilian aircraft near Croydon airport set off air-raid warning sirens. The mass evacuation of schoolchildren, along with mothers expecting babies or with children below school age, began on 1 September. Sandbags were supplied by the government to local authorities, and a blackout was imposed across the country. The use of poison gas in air raids was widely feared; gas masks had been distributed in 1938 and were followed up with leaflets explaining how to gas-proof a room and how to identify different poison gases by smell. Meanwhile, by 9 September the last of thirteen RAF squadrons had deployed to France to support the troops of the BEF; there would be clashes between RAF aircraft and the Luftwaffe over western Germany later in the month, two Fairey Battles and one Messerschmitt being downed over Aachen on 20 September. RAF bombers had also begun to fly raids against German naval targets, attacking Wilhelmshaven, Brunsbuttel and Heligoland.

The Admiralty imposed a convoy system almost immediately after the declaration of war. During the First World War, convoys were not introduced until May 1917, after which shipping losses fell by 90 per cent. Aircraft had successfully been used against U-boats during the First World War: the Blackburn Kangaroo, for instance, which could carry four 250-lb bombs. However, at the start of the Second World War more than half of RAF Coastal Command's strength consisted of Avro Ansons, which could only carry four 100-lb bombs. On 5 September 1939, an Anson attacked a submarine off the east coast of Scotland but the bombs bounced off the water and exploded in mid-air, bringing down the Anson. There was a similar incident later in September when two Skua dive bombers from the aircraft carrier *Ark Royal* attacked U-30; the survivors were picked up by the U-boat and taken prisoner. At the start of the war, only twelve of Coastal Command's Hudsons were equipped with radar, but better sets would be fitted in larger aircraft such as Whitley bombers and Sunderland flying boats. They rarely sank U-boats, although that would change as the war progressed.

The main events of the war in the air in September 1939, however, were on the Eastern Front in Poland. Germany deployed for the first time the tactics of Blitzkrieg, or Lighting War, in which the tanks were closely supported by Junkers Ju-87 Stuka dive-bombers, which acted as airborne artillery, clearing a path for the ground forces. As well as this revolutionary new way of fighting, the Luftwaffe employed a more traditional approach, bombing Warsaw heavily over a number of days in mid-September. The last Polish soldiers in action surrendered on 1 October and Europe moved into the period known as the Phoney War.

A Heinkel 111 bomber became the first German aircraft to be shot down over the British Isles on 28 October. Throughout October, the RAF and Luftwaffe had both launched raids, the RAF making its first night leaflet raid against Berlin at the start of the month, while the Luftwaffe mounted raids against naval targets and convoys off the British coast. The French government had asked Britain not to bomb Germany for fear that the Germans would be provoked into retaliating against French factories. However, the Germans were not so reticent, attacking targets in Scotland including the Forth Bridge and Scapa Flow naval base in Orkney, where the former battleship HMS *Iron Duke* was damaged and had to be beached. On 21 October, the Luftwaffe attacked a British convoy in the North Sea, but were beaten back.

On 13 November the first German bombs of the war hit British soil during an attack on naval vessels and flying boats in the Shetland Islands. Later in the month, German aircraft began a more successful tactic, first dropping magnetic mines in coastal waters and then parachuting them into the Thames Estuary. On the night of 22/23 November, a mine-laying Heinkel 111 jettisoned two magnetic mines off Southend Pier, which gave British experts their first opportunity to examine the new weapon and start to devise counter-measures. In the meantime, mine-laying continued, with one particularly daring seaplane pilot landing in Harwich harbour to plant his mines before taking off again. Incidents like this would spur the development of radar, which could detect low-flying aircraft, something that would prove hugely useful later in the war.

On 30 November, a new front opened in the war when the Soviet Union attacked Finland in response to the latter's refusal to cede strategically important territory near the Soviet border. The first days of the conflict saw heavy Soviet bombing raids on Helsinki in an attempt to destroy Finnish morale. A period of bad weather early in December gave the Finns a respite and an opportunity to properly evacuate Helsinki and to set air-raid precautions such as shelters and firefighting teams.

On 3 December the RAF dropped its first bomb on German soil, accidentally hitting the North Sea island of Heligoland during an attack by Wellington bombers on German shipping. Although none of the bombers was shot down during the raid of 3 December, an attack later in the month by twenty-two Wellingtons was detected by German radar while they were 70 miles off the German coast; with the defences alerted, only ten of the aircraft returned. From 11 December, barrage balloons were regularly seen across Britain. Barrage balloons were intended to serve two purposes: to obscure targets and thus make it less likely that they would be hit, and to force enemy aircraft to fly at a height where they could be hit by anti-aircraft fire. At the end of the month, however, the RAF received a boost as No. 10 squadron of the Royal Australian Air Force arrived on Boxing Day to join Coastal Command, flying Short Sunderland flying boats. No. 10 squadron was the first air force unit from the Dominions (Australia, New Zealand, Canada, and South Africa) to go on active service in Europe. The year ended with the arrest of people celebrating the New Year by shining torches (in contravention of the blackout) onto the statue of Eros in London's Piccadilly Circus.

Build-up

Hermann Göring making a speech. A First World War fighter ace and commander of the famous Richthofen Staffel, Göring was very valuable to the Nazi Party for propaganda purposes. When Hitler came to power in 1933, he gave Göring control over civil and military aviation in Germany.

Germany was banned from developing an air force by the Treaty of Versailles, which ended the First World War. The Treaty of Rapallo of 1922 paved the way for secret military co-operation between Germany and the Soviet Union, including the development of the Luftwaffe. Walther Rathenau signed for Germany. (LoC)

Although Germany was still officially banned from having an air force, boys and young men with an interest in aviation were encouraged and given a basic training in glider clubs. (JC)

The image *below* shows an international glider competition in 1937. That *above* shows the glider owned in the 1930s by the famous German test pilot Hanna Reitsch.

When the military rising that started the Spanish Civil War began, its leader, General Francisco Franco, appealed to Germany for military aid. Franco's emissaries managed to track Hitler down to the Wagner Festival at Bayreuth, and were promised help.

The first military assistance provided by the Germans came in the form of Junkers 52 tri-motor transport aircraft to ferry Spanish Foreign Legion troops loyal to General Franco from North Africa to mainland Spain.

The Condor Legion, the German force in Spain, was equipped with several types of aircraft that the Luftwaffe would later use during the Second World War. *Above* is seen the Heinkel III bomber and *below* the Dornier 17.

Dornier 17z2

The Messerschmitt Bf 109 fighter saw its combat debut during the Spanish Civil War. The 'B' version met its match in the Polikarov I-16 'Rata' monoplane fighters provided to the Republicans by the Soviet Union, and lessons from the Me 109B's combat experience in Spain were incorporated into the Me 109E, widely used by the Luftwaffe during the Second World War.

The Junkers 87 Stuka dive-bomber also saw its combat debut during the Spanish Civil War, where it was found to be an extremely effective weapon for the war that the Nationalist army wanted the Condor Legion to fight.

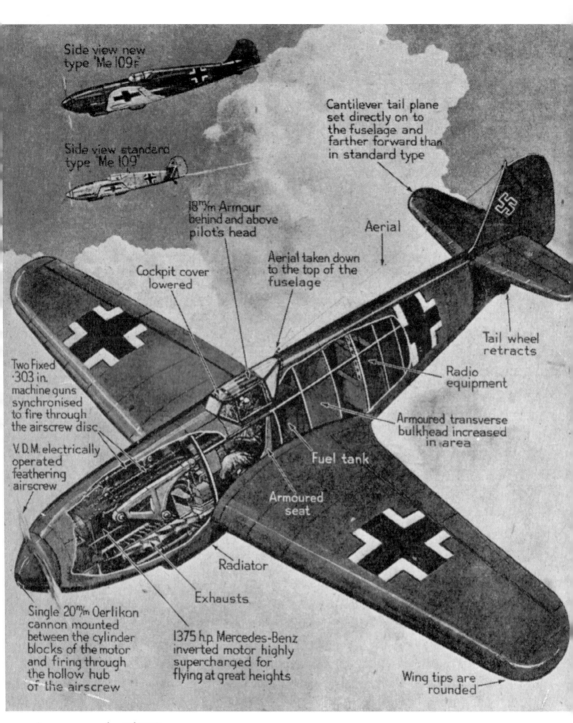

Side view new type "Me 109F"

Side view standard type "Me 109"

Cantilever tail plane set directly on to the fuselage and farther forward than in standard type

18 m/m Armour behind and above pilot's head

Aerial taken down to the top of the fuselage

Aerial

Cockpit cover lowered

Tail wheel retracts

Two Fixed ·303 in. machine guns synchronised to fire through the airscrew disc.

Radio equipment

V.D.M. electrically operated feathering airscrew

Armoured transverse bulkhead increased in area

Fuel tank

Armoured seat

Radiator

Exhausts

Single 20 m/m Oerlikon cannon mounted between the cylinder blocks of the motor and firing through the hollow hub of the airscrew

1375 h.p. Mercedes-Benz inverted motor highly supercharged for flying at great heights

Wing tips are rounded

A cutaway of a Bf 109.

A single-engined Japanese Army bomber on a reconnaissance flight over the Yangtze valley. The winding river can clearly be seen. In autumn 1938 Japanese forces drove up the Yangtze towards the industrial city of Wuhan, which fell on 25 October 1938.

The *Kaga* conducting air operations in 1937. In August of that year *Kaga* began to operate in the East China Sea, her aircraft supporting Japanese military operations along the central Chinese coast and around Shanghai. (Wikipedia)

The standard Japanese Army twin-engined bomber, introduced in 1938. Aircraft such as these mounted the air raid on Chiang Kai-shek's capital at Chungking; the city's population was swollen with refugees from all over China and the bombers attacked as people came home from work.

Opposite top: The aircraft carrier *Kaga* conducting air operations in 1930. In 1932, *Kaga* was deployed to the Chinese coast and her aircraft operated both from the carrier itself and from an airfield outside Shanghai in support of Japanese troops fighting in the city. (Wikipedia)

Opposite bottom: Three of the *Kaga*'s fighter pilots pose in front of a Nakajima A1N2 fighter after the mission on which they scored the Imperial Japanese Navy's first aerial combat victory on 22 February 1932, while supporting Japanese troops on the ground in China. (Wikipedia)

The Bristol Bulldog served as a fighter with the RAF from 1929 until July 1937, when it was replaced by another biplane fighter, the Gloster Gauntlet.

GLOSTER I (LANDPLANE TYPE)

The Gloster Gladiator, which came into service in 1937, was a replacement for the Gauntlet, although it too was a biplane at a time when monoplanes were proving their worth in combat in Spain.

As the Second World War drew closer, the RAF had no operational heavy bombers, only medium bombers like the Vickers Wellington seen here, which was designed by Barnes Wallis. Built using a geodesic construction (an aluminium alloy frame covered with layers of linen treated with dope), the Wellington came into service in 1938.

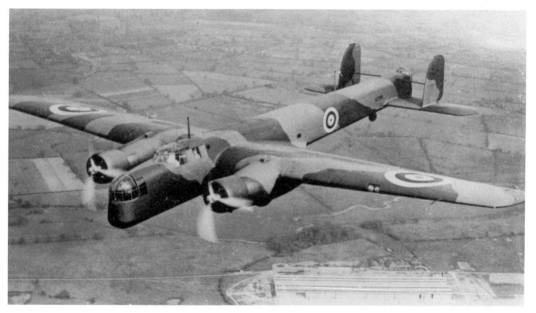

The Armstrong Whitworth Whitley was another of the RAF's medium bombers, introduced in 1937, and was used to drop propaganda leaflets over Germany on the first night of the war. However, it was obsolete when the war started and incapable of facing the German defences with any hope of survival.

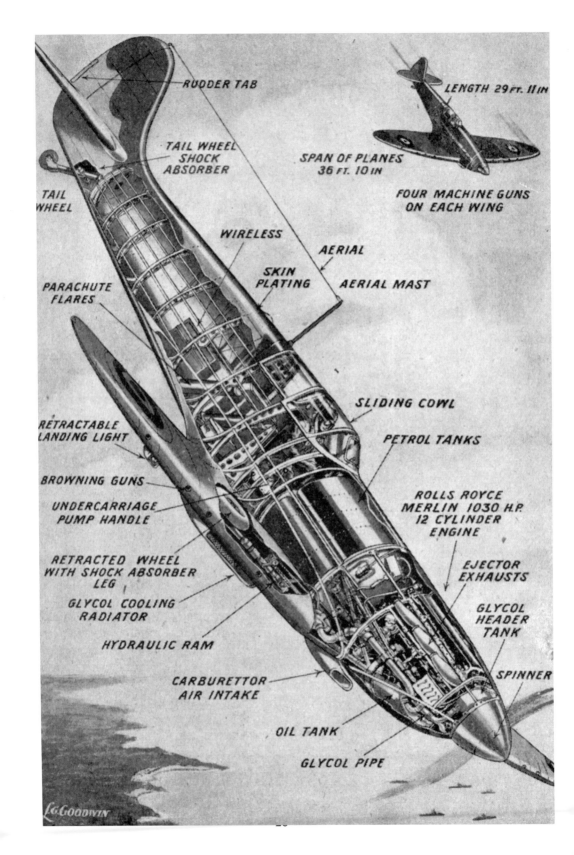

RUDDER TAB

TAIL WHEEL SHOCK ABSORBER

TAIL WHEEL

WIRELESS

SKIN PLATING

AERIAL

AERIAL MAST

PARACHUTE FLARES

RETRACTABLE LANDING LIGHT

BROWNING GUNS

UNDERCARRIAGE PUMP HANDLE

RETRACTED WHEEL WITH SHOCK ABSORBER LEG

GLYCOL COOLING RADIATOR

HYDRAULIC RAM

CARBURETTOR AIR INTAKE

OIL TANK

GLYCOL PIPE

SLIDING COWL

PETROL TANKS

ROLLS ROYCE MERLIN 1030 H.P. 12 CYLINDER ENGINE

EJECTOR EXHAUSTS

GLYCOL HEADER TANK

SPINNER

LENGTH 29 FT. 11 IN

SPAN OF PLANES 36 FT. 10 IN

FOUR MACHINE GUNS ON EACH WING

L.G. GOODWIN

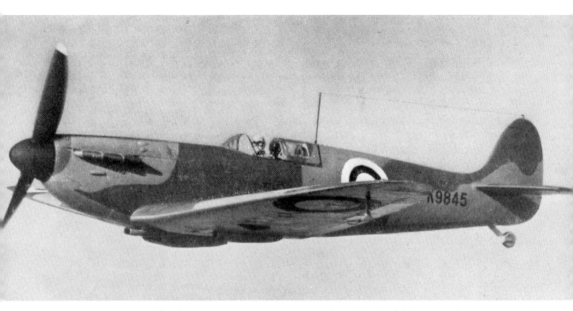

The Supermarine Spitfire began coming into service with operational RAF squadrons in 1938. A modern metal monoplane, it meant that with the Hawker Hurricane (which entered service in 1937) Fighter Command had aircraft that could take on the German Bf 109s.

Opposite page: A cutaway image of a Spitfire.

September 1939

Part of the German Blitzkrieg: a Polish armoured train is seen here derailed by the dropping of two 520-lb bombs on the railway line. Aerial attacks such as these seriously hampered Polish efforts to defend themselves.

The Polish fort at Modlin, to the north of Warsaw, is seen in these two photographs. *Above*, smoke is seen rising after an aerial attack while on the *right* we see the effects of the bombing on the fort's buildings.

Luftwaffe Junkers Ju 87 Stuka dive-bombers flying over Poland, and civilian casualties which resulted from an attack on the village of Krzemieniec on 25 September.

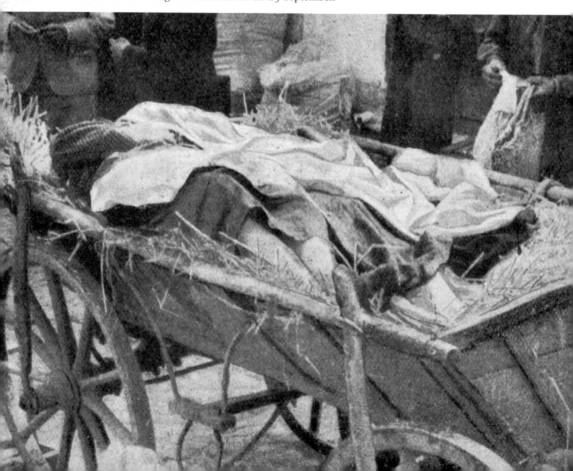

Above left: A casualty of the air raids is seen here receiving medical attention.

Above right: The ruins of a block of flats in the Warsaw suburbs after the city had been bombed by the Luftwaffe.

Above: Another image showing the bombing of the Warsaw suburbs; this time the effects of German incendiary bombs are seen.

Opposite top: Mothers and children leaving London. A mass evacuation from British cities was carried out during the first days of September.

Opposite bottom: What was left when it was all over: the ruins of a house on the outskirts of Warsaw following a raid on the city.

A nurse at a welfare centre registers the details of a mother and child evacuated from London.

Opposite top: A stretcher case being lifted into a makeshift ambulance, formerly a Green Line coach, during evacuation.

Opposite bottom: During September, 200 London schools were open for further registration of children whose parents wanted them to be evacuated.

Schoolchildren evacuated to a town on the South Coast are seen asking a steel-helmeted policeman the way to their new school.

Children evacuated from Liverpool are seen at Formby, on the Lancashire coast, helping to fill sandbags.

An air-raid warden trains by carrying a female 'casualty' to safety.

A uniformed London policeman wearing his gas mask. One of the major fears of the British authorities was that gas would be used against the civilian population.

WANDSWORTH A.R.P.

GAS
DETECTION

WANDSWORTH A.R.

AIR RAI
WARDEN

More prosaic precautions. This image and the image overleaf show ARP shelters being tested for strength; they have been placed under a wall, which is then knocked down on top of them.

Opposite top: A way of warning against gas attack: the piece of paper on this sentry's bayonet would change colour in the presence of mustard gas.

Opposite bottom: A section of men being instructed in gas drill, which apparently included being trained to recognise different gases by smell using samples of the real thing!

Opposite top: An anti-aircraft gun position being prepared in one of the London parks.

Opposite bottom: A Swedish-designed Bofors anti-aircraft gun.

This device was designed to detect the sound of approaching enemy aircraft. It is seen being demonstrated to the king and queen at Chobham.

Opposite top: An anti-aircraft gun crew training using a predictor to follow a moving target.

Opposite bottom: Training using a miniature searchlight in a drill hall.

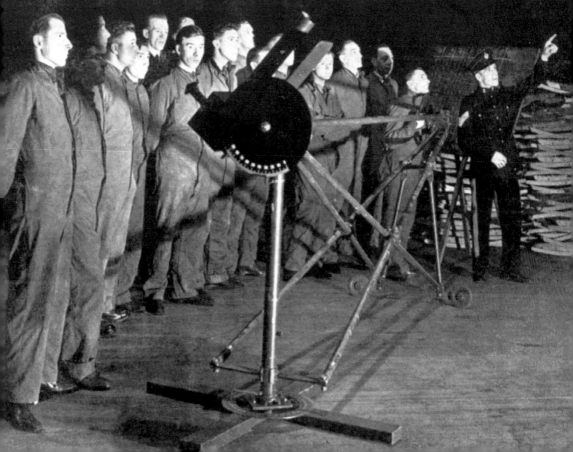

Practising with a real searchlight.

Opposite top: Fairey Battle light bombers. Several squadrons of these aircraft were despatched to France as part of the Advanced Air Striking Force (AASF) and they were kept strictly under the control of the RAF – the Army had no say in their use.

Opposite bottom: Westland Lysander army co-operation aircraft over Hampshire. Lysanders too were deployed to France to support the BEF, although the RAF's army co-operation squadrons had been neglected before the war.

Fighter support for the BEF would be supplied by Hawker Hurricanes, as seen here.

RAF pilots with the BEF in France studying maps before setting out on a reconnaissance mission.

An RAF observer hands photographic plates to a member of the ground crew after returning from a reconnaissance flight.

An aerial photograph of the Kiel Canal, which was attacked by RAF bombers on 4 September.

These two images show the start of the RAF bombing mission against the Kiel Canal. The upper image shows the Wing Commander waving goodbye and good luck to the Squadron Leader leading the raid. The image *below* shows one of the bombers taking off from the airfield. These photographs were both used as part of the film *The Lion Has Wings*.

Two more images from *The Lion Has Wings*. The image *above* is a studio reconstruction of aircrew at their stations on board one of the aircraft en route to Germany. The image *below* shows the actual return of aircrew from the raid; one of the pilots is seen smoking a cigarette on his return to base.

The aircraft works at Friedrichshafen, which were bombed by aircraft of the French air force on 24 September. These are the former Zeppelin hangars, cut down for reuse. Zeppelin later made components for V-2 rockets.

Opposite page: Flying Officer Andrew McPherson and Flying Officer Kenneth Doran, both of whom were awarded the DFC on 2 November for their part in the raid on the Kiel Canal.

The naval base of Heligoland in the North Sea, attacked by the RAF on 29 September.

Opposite top: A reconnaissance photograph of the Saar Valley in western Germany; it was taken on one of the RAF's flights over enemy territory.

Opposite bottom: An RAF Short Singapore flying boat on patrol against U-boats at the mouth of the River Thames.

RAF Anson reconnaissance aircraft on patrol with destroyers.

This photograph, taken from the freighter SS *American Farmer*, shows a Royal Navy Fairey Swordfish aircraft searching for the U-boat that had just sunk the British freighter *Kafiristan*. The crew can just be seen scanning the sea for signs of the U-boat.

October 1939

London civil defence chief Admiral Sir Edward Evans watching an unrehearsed ARP exercise and, *opposite*, speaking to one of the volunteers while the 'air raid' was in progress.

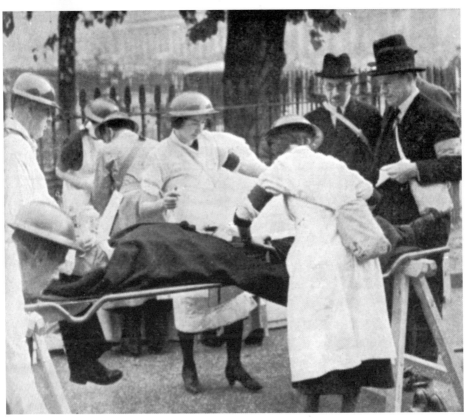

A casualty clearing station where 'wounded' volunteers are given first aid before being taken to hospital, and first aid workers dressing a casualty in the street.

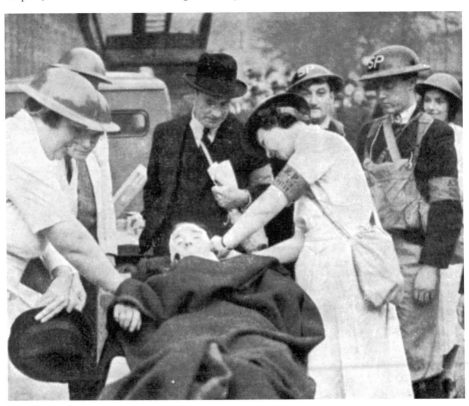

Auxiliary Fire Service (AFS) men practising putting out a fire in the Surrey Commercial Docks in East London.

Above: The Forth Bridge, attacked by German bombers on 16 October 1939. Consequently, it was one of the first targets outside of London to be protected by barrage balloons.

Left: A photograph of the Forth Bridge and shipping in the Firth of Forth published in the *Berliner Illustrirte Zeitung* and said to have been taken by one of the German pilots on the raid.

In a second German air raid on Scotland, HMS *Iron Duke*, a decommissioned battleship used as a training ship, was attacked.

The coffins of two German aircrew who were killed in the attacks against Scotland are borne through the streets by an RAF honour guard and are seen overleaf, buried draped in Swastika flags in a cemetery near Edinburgh.

Female workers painting 'dope' onto fabric for the wings of bombers in an aircraft factory. Aircraft dope is a lacquer that stiffens and tightens fabric around an airframe as well as making it airtight and waterproof. Many doping agents are highly flammable.

Workers constructing the fuselage of a bomber in another part of the factory.

A flight of Allied reconnaissance aircraft over the Western Front.

A Women's Auxiliary Air Force (WAAF) section leader on parade at an RAF station.

Members of the WAAF on parade in Lancashire.

Opposite bottom and p. 62: Sound location equipment and searchlight in use.

Female members of the Auxiliary Fire Service stand by to take emergency calls in the telephone control room of a London fire station.

On 28 October 1939 the first enemy aircraft of the war to fall on British soil was shot down over southern Scotland. A Heinkel He 111, it became known as the Humbie Heinkel, after the village near where it came down. *Above*, a crowd gathers around the crash site, on which guards have been posted. *Below*, experts from the RAF examine the wreckage.

Cases of machine-gun ammunition recovered from the wreckage of the Humbie Heinkel.

1. An illustration of an air exercise from the July 1936 issue of *Popular Flying*. The aircraft in the foreground is a Hawker Demon; the three in the background are Gloster Gauntlets. This illustration is roughly contemporary with the start of the Spanish Civil War, in which biplanes would be outshone by monoplanes. (JC)

2. This image of an RAF bomber, possibly a Handley-Page Harrow, comes from the cover of the October 1937 issue of *Popular Flying*. The Harrow was only phased out as a bomber at the end of 1939, as more modern aircraft became available. (JC)

3. K4636 was the first production Hawker Hind and first flew on 4 September 1935. The Hind served as a light bomber with the RAF between 1935 and 1938, being replaced by the Fairey Battle and Bristol Blenheim. It is shown here on the cover of the 19 July 1938 issue of *Wonders of World Aviation* magazine. (JC)

4. This image from the cover of the December 1937 issue of *Popular Flying* shows a flight of British bombers, possibly Bristol Blenheims; the Blenheim first came into service in 1937 and although it could survive against the biplane fighters still in use in the late 1930s, it could not against more modern aircraft like the Bf 109. (JC)

PART 6   ALL-METAL CONSTRUCTION

WONDERS OF WORLD AVIATION

7D
WEEKLY

TO BE COMPLETED
IN ABOUT
45 WEEKLY PARTS

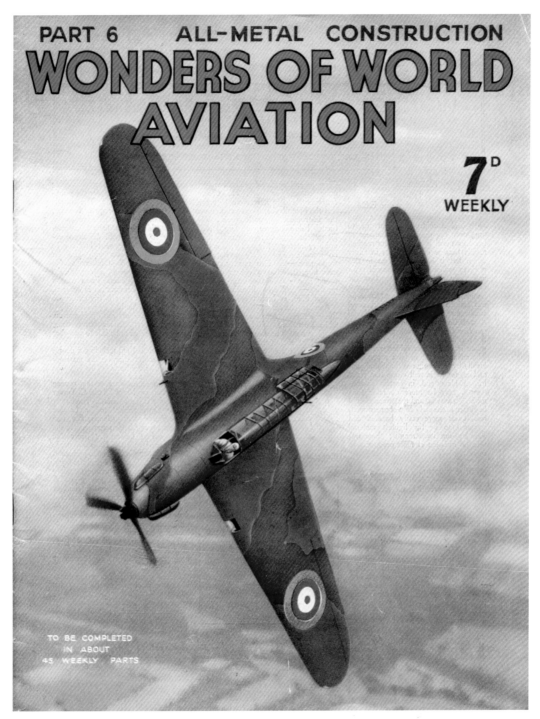

5. The Fairey Battle was the standard RAF light bomber when the Second World War began. The Advanced Air Striking Force, sent to France as part of the BEF in September 1939, was equipped with Battles. (JC)

6. This illustration from June 1939 shows a flight of Hawker Hurricane fighters at an air show. The Hurricane had first flown in November 1935 and entered into service with the RAF in 1937. (JC)

7/8. Both of these two images shows a Westland Lysander army co-operation aircraft. The image above, from the May 1939 *Popular Flying*, shows a Lysander operating with two tanks; the image below, from *Wonders of World Aviation*, is a close-up. The RAF top brass were not keen on the idea of army co-operation. (JC)

9. A hangover from the First World War, the Germans continued to use balloons for observation purposes. (JC)

10. In contrast, the British balloon barrage was unmanned and entirely defensive. (JC)

11. This advert from early December 1939 shows the extent to which barrage balloons had become a part of everyday life in Britain within three months of the outbreak of war. (JC)

12. German seaplanes like this Ar 196 were used to lay magnetic mines in British coastal waters. (AA)

13. A head-on view of a German sea-plane taking off on a mission. (AA)

14. A Heinkel He 115 sea-plane on a mission to lay magnetic mines in British waters. (AA)

15. A Luftwaffe Staffelkapitän in front of his Dornier Do 17. (AA)

16. A German bomber crew preparing to leave on a mission. (AA)

17. German pilots studying a map before taking off. (AA)

18. A view out of the nose of a He 111 bomber on a flight over the North Sea. (AA)

19. A formation of Junkers Ju 87 Stuka dive bombers in flight. The Stuka's effectiveness as a ground support aircraft was proven in Spain, and later in Poland. (AA)

20/21 Two views of Messerschmitt Bf 109s on the ground, with their ground crews working on them. (AA)

An RAF officer gesturing towards the bullet holes left by the fighter pilots who eventually brought down the Heinkel.

The wreckage of a German He 111 bomber brought down by RAF fighters on the Western Front in France.

A group of French air force officers pose with the black cross taken from a German Messerschmitt fighter which had been forced down over France.

Beneath this corrugated iron structure is the statue of King Charles I in Whitehall. It was covered up to protect it from damage during air raids.

The entrance to Mansion House station in the City of London, one of the London Underground stations converted to be used as a public air-raid shelter.

The Dominions, as they then were, Australia, Canada, New Zealand and South Africa, had also declared war on Germany in September 1939. These two images show pilots in training for the Royal Australian Air Force at Kingsford-Smith aerodrome, Sydney.

Above is another image showing the training of RAAF aircrew; these recruits are learning about how aircraft engines work. To the right, we see a pilot and observer from the Royal Canadian Air Force getting ready for a training flight.

WARNUNG!

England an das deutsche Volk

Die Nazi-Regierung hat, trotz der Bemühungen der führenden Großmächte, die Welt in einen Krieg gestürzt.

Dieser Krieg ist ein Verbrechen. Das deutsche Volk muß zwischen dem Vorwand, den seine Regierung benutzt, um den Krieg vom Zaun zu brechen und den Grundsätzen, die England und Frankreich zur Verteidigung Polens zwingen, ganz klar unterscheiden.

Von Anfang an hat die englische Regierung erklärt, daß an der polnischen Frage nichts ist, was einen europäischen Krieg mit allen seinen tragischen Folgen rechtfertigen kann.

Fünf Monate nach dem Münchener Vertrag wurde die Selbstständigkeit der Tschechoslovakei brutal zertreten. Wenn Polen nicht auch von dem gleichen Schicksal erreicht werden soll, dann mußten wir darauf bestehen, daß friedliche Verhandlungsmethoden nicht durch Gewaltandrohungen unmöglich gemacht werden, daß die zu treffende Abmachung die Lebensrechte Polens gewährleistet und auch ehrlich gehalten wird. Ein Diktat konnten wir weder zulaßen noch annehmen.

Wenn Herr Hitler glaubte, die englische Regierung werde aus Angst vor dem Kriege die Polen im Stich laßen, so hat er sich schwer getäuscht. Erstens bricht England sein einmal gegebenes Wort nicht. Außerdem ist es aber Zeit, der brutalen Gewalt, die die Nazi-Regierung der Welt aufzwingen will, ein deutliches Halt zu bieten.

Mit diesem Krieg stellt sich der Reichskanzler gegen den unbeugsamen Willen der englischen Regierung, einen Willen, hinter dem nicht nur die gesamten Hilfsquellen und Mittel des englischen

A reproduction of one of the leaflets dropped by the RAF over Germany. The heading at the top reads: 'Warning: A Message from Great Britain'.

November 1939

ARP drills continue as Britain prepares itself. *Above*, crowds can be seen watching from a distance as ARP wardens deal with the aftermath of a 'raid' on Bethnal Green. *Overleaf*, AFS personnel practise using the powerful hoses aboard a firefighting launch on the Thames.

Left: A patrol boat of the Emergency River Service.

Opposite: An ARP warden on duty.

The effects of the blackout in Piccadilly Circus, *above*,
and Regent Street, where newly introduced starlight street
lighting can be seen.

A pedestrian crosses the road at night in the blackout wearing a white coat and carrying a newspaper.

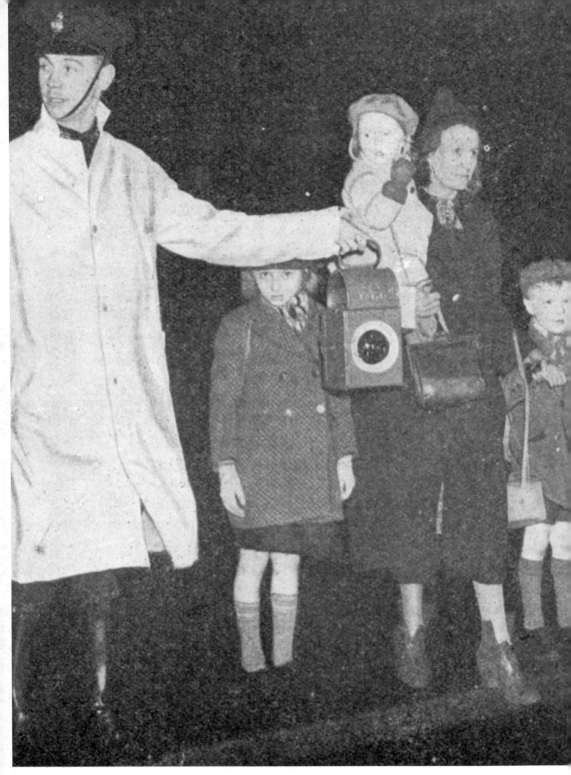

A white-coated policeman with a lantern ushers pedestrians across the road in Trafford Bar, Manchester.

New street lighting in Liverpool, *top*, which cannot be seen more than 30 feet above the ground. *Right* is seen one of the new reading lights installed in a blacked-out train carriage.

French naval and air assets played their part in trying to keep the Atlantic sea lanes open during the early months of the war. *Above* can be seen a squadron of French seaplanes preparing to take off on patrol. *Below* is a French flying boat accompanying French destroyers at sea.

A typical convoy far out at sea.

A Fairey Swordfish torpedo bomber on patrol over a convoy, watching for U-boats.

These photos show part of the reason why keeping the sea lanes open was so important for Britain and France. Both Allied powers had placed large orders for military aircraft with firms in the US to supplement their own production. *Above:* Wings for an order of bombers for the RAF in the Lockheed plant in California. *Below:* Air-cooled radial engines for another Allied order being tested at the North American Aviation plant, also in California.

A completed Hudson outside the factory, ready for delivery. Note the obscured RAF markings on the side of the fuselage.

Fuselages for Hudson reconnaissance bombers at the Lockheed plant in California.

A Hudson wrapped in a protective cover being loaded aboard a ship for transport to Britain.

Hudsons, still in their protective wrapping but with their RAF markings and camouflage paint applied, wait on the quayside for onwards transport.

A Short Singapore flying boat of RAF Coastal Command about to be launched at its base, *above*, and taking off, *opposite*. Patrols by long-range flying boats would prove to be of vital importance in tackling the German U-boats.

The Observer Corps in action. At posts across the UK, members of the Observer Corps watched for approaching enemy aircraft, calculating their altitude and course. They were well equipped with material to help them identify enemy aircraft and, more importantly, to distinguish between enemy aircraft and friendly ones, as seen overleaf.

Barrage balloons being tested. In the image *above*, the stabiliser for a balloon is being inflated as part of a final test before it leaves the factory. In the image *below*, a complete balloon is being inflated in front of an audience of female workers at the factory.

Mechanics overhauling a French air force Dewoitine D. 520 fighter after a heavy day of fighting over the Western Front.

More aerial battles took place over the Western Front on 21 November. Here, men from the French air force are seen examining the wreckage of two of the German aircraft that were brought down: *above* is a wrecked German He 111 bomber, *below* a reconnaissance aircraft.

Opposite bottom: The fuselage of a downed German He 111 bomber being towed through a French village after it had been shot down over the French lines.

A search being carried out of the wreckage of a Luftwaffe Heinkel bomber, which had been shot down over the Meuse district of eastern France. *Below* is an American-made Curtiss P-36 fighter of the French air force on patrol over the Western Front.

These images show nine French fighters in formation, *above*, and two of the French fighters in a dogfight with six Messerschmitts, *below*. Nine German aircraft of a force of twenty-seven were claimed shot down.

These two images show an RAF fighter pursuing a German bomber, *above*, and the crashed He 111 bomber in a field near Hazebrouck.

SILENCE

A reconstruction of the Fighter Command Central Control Room from the film *The Lion Has Wings*. Orders are issued to scramble the fighters from the gallery while the position, course, speed and number of enemy aircraft are plotted on the table.

An Observer Corps Control Centre, where reports of incoming enemy aircraft from Observer Corps posts are plotted.

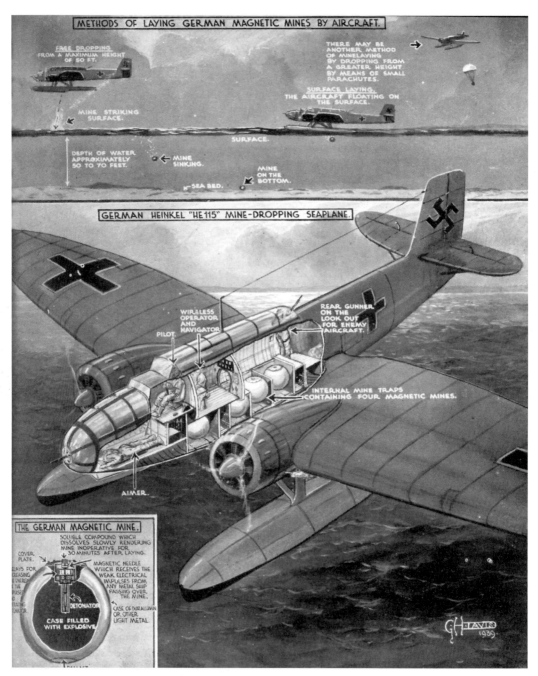

A diagram taken from the *Illustrated London News* showing the use of seaplanes in laying fields of magnetic mines off the British coast.

The seaplane base at Borkum in the Frisian Islands, which lie along the North Sea coasts of Germany and the Netherlands, seen before the war with Heinkel He 60 seaplanes drawn up at the water's edge. It was from here that many of the mine-laying missions set off, and on 28 November RAF fighters attacked the base in an attempt to stop them.

A diagram of a magnetic mine, also taken from the *Illustrated London News*. When a metal ship passes over it, a magnetic needle in the mine moves, building up the electrical charge needed to set off the explosive.

The so-called Winter War between Finland and the Soviet Union began on 30 November 1939 after the Finns had refused to agree to Stalin's territorial demands. The opening day of the invasion involved heavy bombing raids by the Soviet air force against Helsinki, the results of which can be seen in these images.

At the end of November, thousands of the inhabitants of Helsinki, fearing that negotiations with the Soviet Union would not end in peace, left the city by train for fear of air raids. This image shows a crowd waiting on the platform of the central station.

The queue continued outside Helsinki railway station.

An official government building in Helsinki being protected from bomb damage using sandbags.

Hastily prepared trenches in the open spaces of Helsinki.

December 1939

South African Air Force reconnaissance aircraft setting off on a patrol of the Atlantic coast of South Africa.

Above: The German liner *Watussi*, on fire and sinking after being scuttled on 2 December. *Watussi* was intercepted by South African aircraft looking for German armed merchant cruisers (merchant ships armed with naval guns), which had been a serious worry to the Royal Navy.

Right: A German seaplane being fuelled for its next mission, which is believed to have been a flight to lay a magnetic mine off the British coast.

Fleet Air Arm pilots examining the course for a training flight at HMS *Peregrine*.

Fleet Air Arm observers taking down final instructions before taking off on a flight.

A Fleet Air Arm air crew leaving a Supermarine Walrus biplane after a flight.

The wreckage of a twin-engined Heinkel reconnaissance aircraft washed up on the beach at Sheringham, Norfolk. The wreckage is being examined by RAF personnel. It was thought that the aircraft had been laying mines.

These two images show a barrage
balloon being raised over the Thames
Estuary, and a raised balloon tethered
to a barge in the estuary. Barrage
balloons were partly intended to
discourage low-flying aircraft; many
of the German mine-laying aircraft
deliberately flew low.

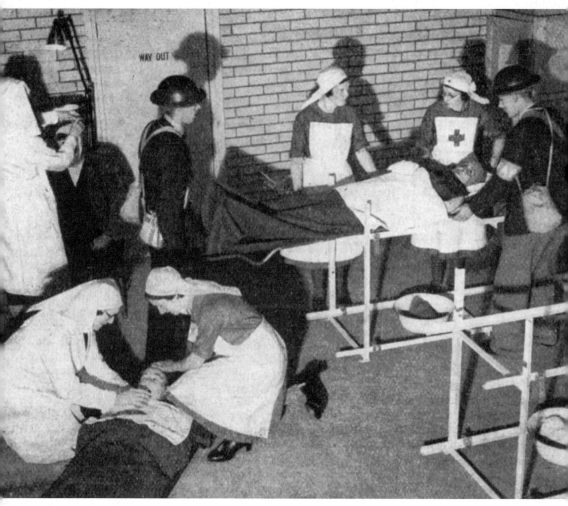

Members of the VAD at work in an underground emergency hospital built by the borough council in Erith, Kent, during an ARP exercise.

The fore-deck of the Grimsby trawler *Etruria*, which was bombed by German aircraft in the North Sea. Three of the *Etruria*'s crew were killed and one was injured; the survivors are seen below.

This image, from Scandinavian sources, shows an attack from the air on a trawler.

An RAF Fairey Battle light bomber at a forward airfield in eastern France.

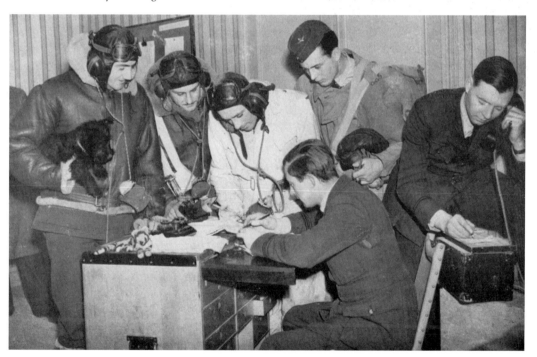

RAF aircrew in France being briefed before taking off on their mission.

The island of Heligoland in the North Sea. The German naval base that can be seen in the foreground was the target of an RAF mission on 18 December.

These two images show some of the RAF aircraft (Wellington bombers) and aircrew who flew the mission over Heligoland.

Damage caused by continuing Soviet air raids over Finland. These two images show the town of Viipuri, now Vyborg in Russia; the image *above* shows the destruction in a working-class area and the image *below* shows a bomb-damaged restaurant.

These two images show more of the build-up of armed forces in the Dominions. The image *above* shows Hawker Hind aircraft lined up on a South African airfield ready for a flight. *Below*, cadets from the RAAF are seen on their way to the first lesson of the day.

These images show the training of aircrew in Canada. The image *above* shows a trainee pilot at the controls of an Oxford bomber, preparing to take off from the airfield at Trenton, Ontario. The image *left* shows an RCAF student loading practice bombs on to the bomb racks of a training aircraft.

A Fairey Battle light bomber taking off from a RCAF training airfield.

Children watching rescue workers among wrecked buildings in Vaasa following a Soviet air raid in which about 300 bombs were thought to have been dropped.

Although Soviet air raids deliberately targeted some Finnish towns and cities, other communities, such as the village seen here, were damaged as part of Soviet attacks on Finnish road and rail communications.

Soviet aircraft over Helsinki.

An air-raid warden on top of a tall building in Helsinki watches for Soviet aircraft.

A Messerschmitt Bf 109 fighter shot down by French anti-aircraft guns while on a reconnaissance mission over eastern France.

Another Bf 109, shot down by a French fighter, is seen on show to the public in Paris.

The wreckage of a Dornier Do 17 bomber which had been shot down in eastern France by French fighter aircraft.

The first RAAF squadron to come to Britain arrived on 26 December, and was deployed to RAF Coastal Command. The men are seen *above* studying a map and pulling a Short Sunderland flying boat into position, *right*.

On patrol in a Sunderland flying boat somewhere over the Atlantic. *Above*, one pilot operates the control while the other uses an Aldis lamp to pass signals in Morse code. *Opposite*, the gunners midships man their posts.

RAF pilots in flying kit walking towards their Fairey Battle aircraft, which are lined up on an airfield in France, ready for an early morning flight.

RAF aircraft deployed on forward airfields in France during the winter of 1939/40. *Above*, ground crew are seen taking the tarpaulin off the cockpit of an aircraft and clearing the snow off the wings. *Below*, an RAF sentry guards an aircraft with a protective cover over the engine.

Testing the guns of an RAF Spitfire at a depot in Britain. *Above*, the ground crew load a belt of ammunition into one of the wing-mounted machine guns and, *opposite*, fire the guns at a target; empty cartridge cases can be seen falling to the ground underneath the wings.

Hitler mounted a tour of inspection along the Western Front over Christmas 1939. He is seen here addressing Luftwaffe personnel at an airfield behind the front line.